Dream
Big

You
Are
Enough

You
Get
What
You
Give

Protect
Your
Inner
Peace

Be The
Change
You Want
To See

Aim For The Finish Line

Just
Be
You

Prove
Them
Wrong

Keep Trying

Always
Stay
Humble

Be Kind
All The
Time

Always
Wear A
Smile

Being
Happy
Is A
Choice

Believe
You
Can

It Is
Never
Too
Late

Give It
All
Your
Heart

Be
Faithful
To
Yourself

Dare
To
Fail

Keep
Going
Be
All In

The
Journey
Begins
With One
Step

Give
It All
You
Have
Got

Do Small
Things
In A
Great
Way

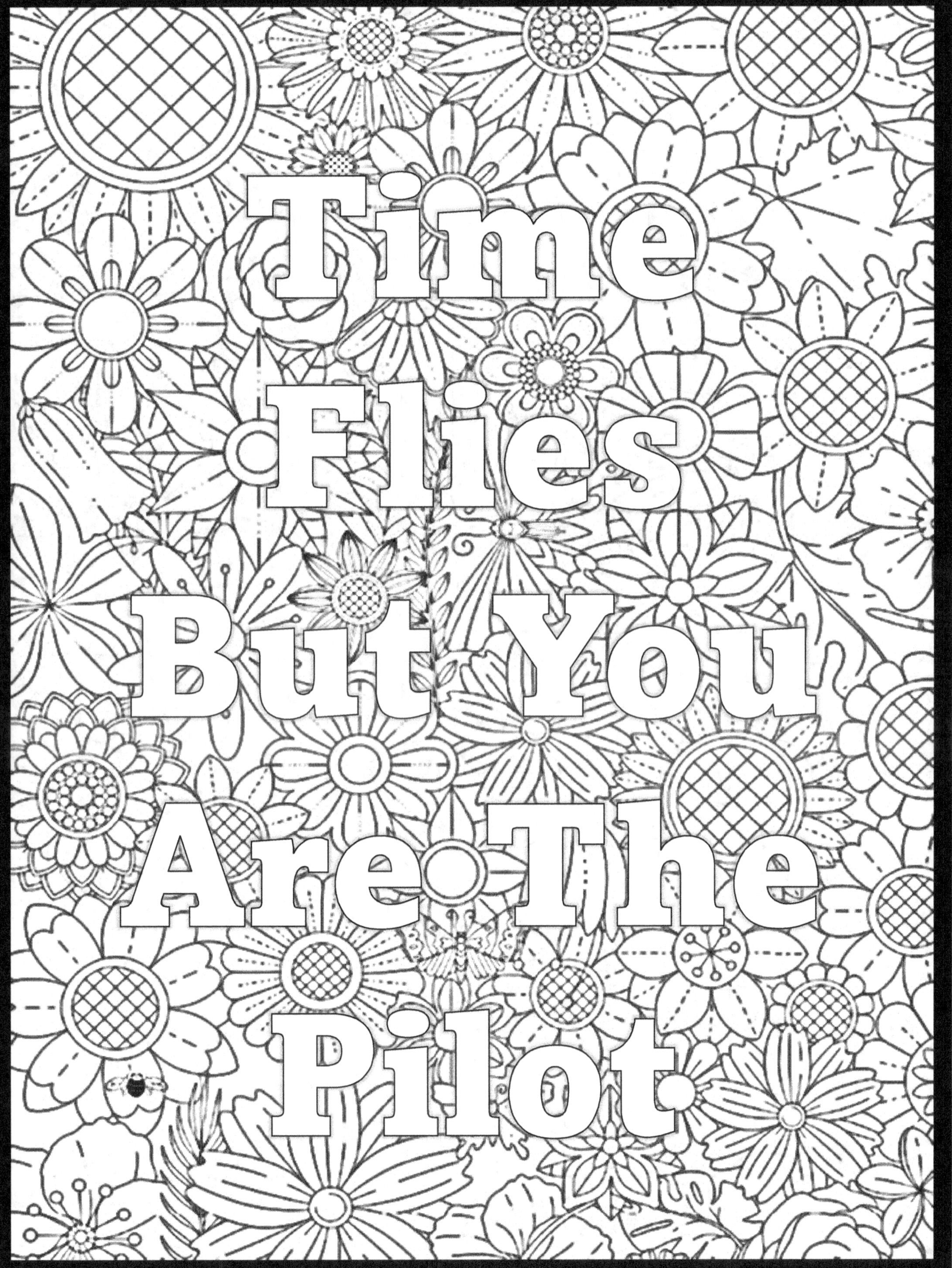

Time
Flies
But You
Are The
Pilot

Be A
Rainbow
In
Someone's
Cloud

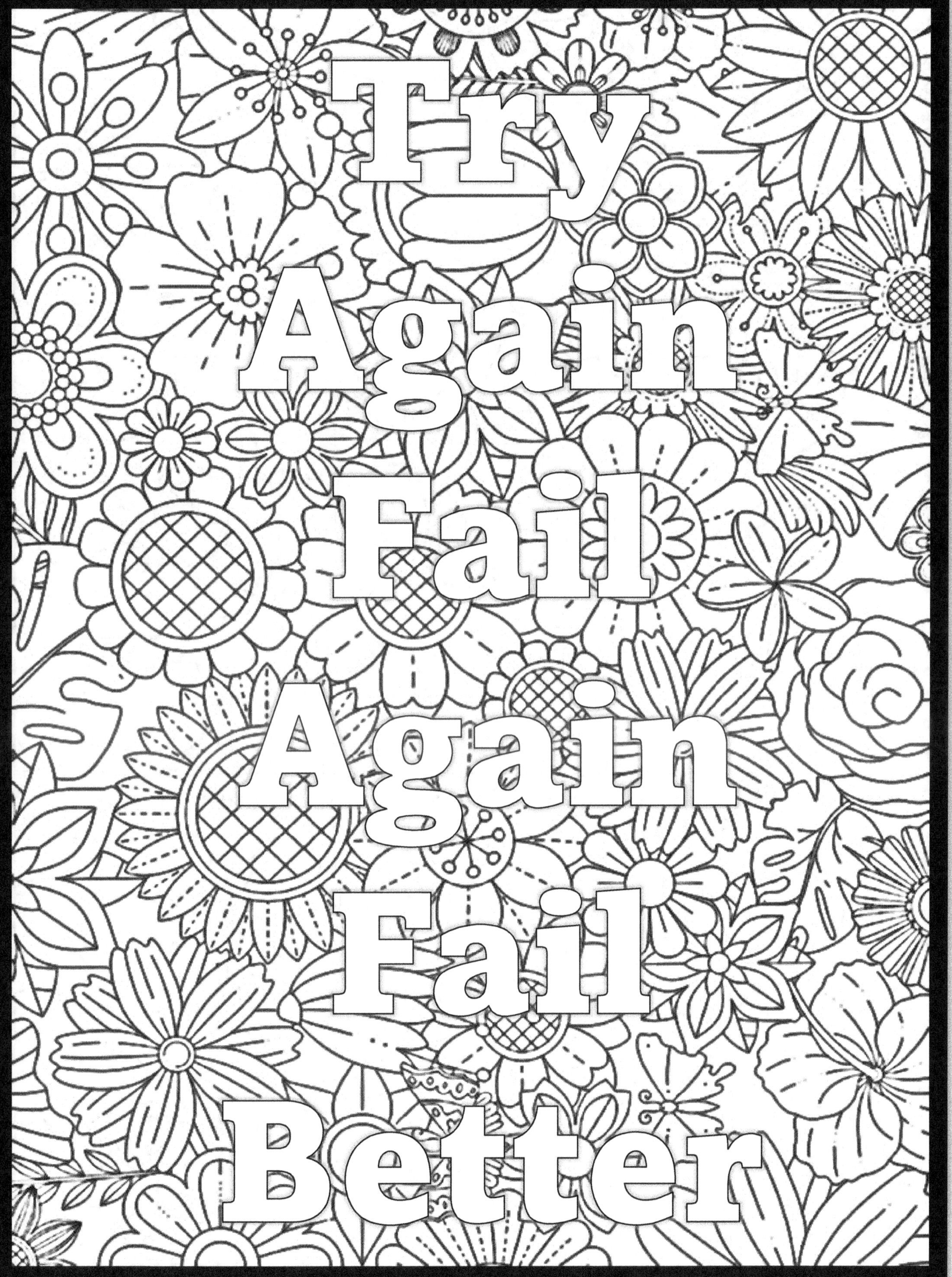
Try
Again
Fail
Again
Fail
Better

You Can
If You
Think
You Can

Be
Yourself
Everyone
Else Is
Already
Taken

Open
Your
Mind

You Never Fail Until You Stop Trying

Life Is
About
Creating
Yourself

Create
Your
Own
Sunshine

Take Time
To Do
What
Makes
You
Happy

Begin
Anywhere
Just
Begin

Life Is
Really
Simple

Live Your Dreams

Find
Your
Own
Path

Be
Afraid
To
Stand
Still

Start
Your
Day
Determined

End
Your
Day
Satisfied

Determine
Your
Priorities

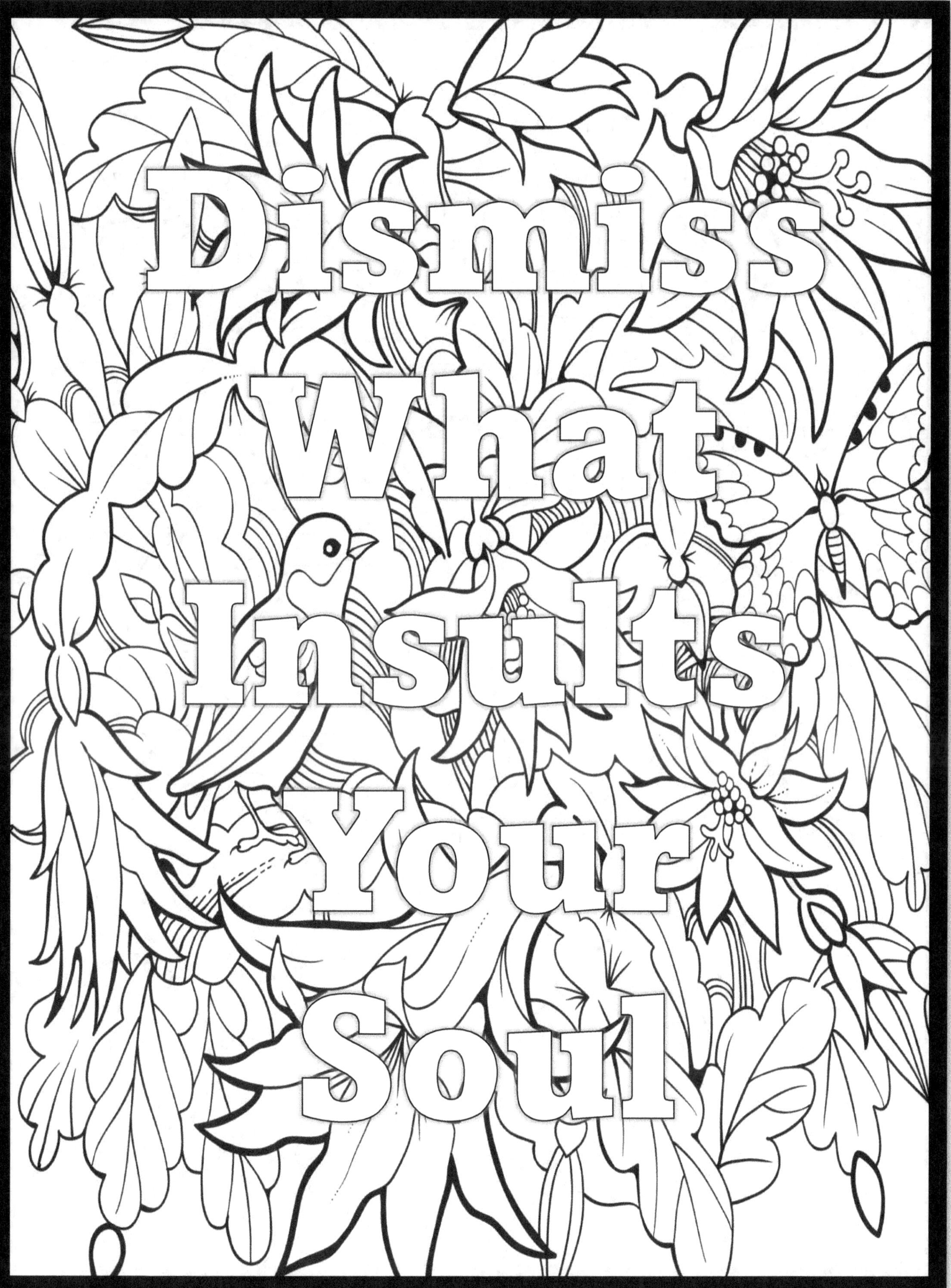
Dismiss What Insults Your Soul

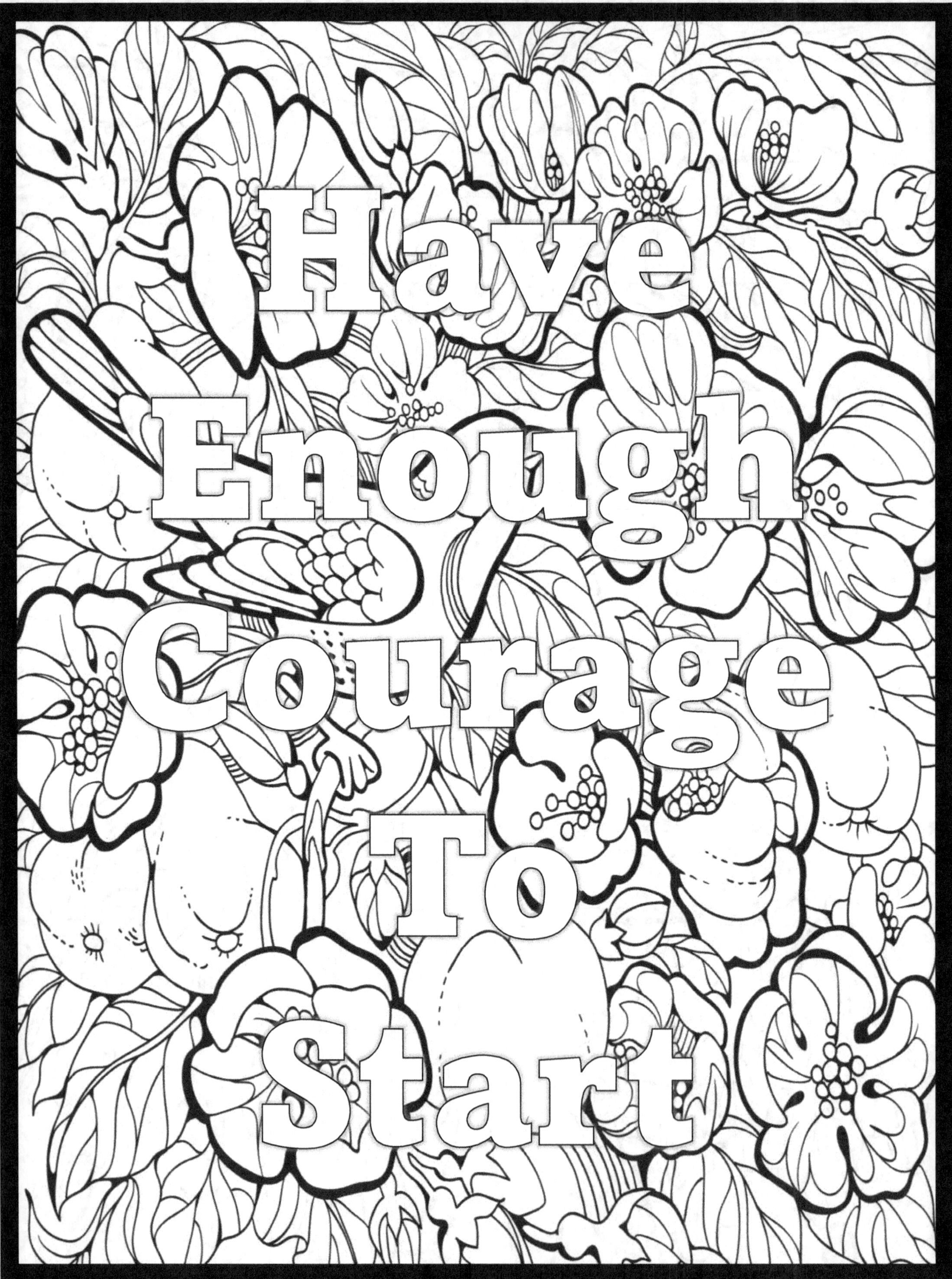
Have
Enough
Courage
To
Start

Have
Enough
Heart
To
Finish

Be So
Good
They
Cannot
Ignore
You

Mistakes
Help
You
Grow

Imperfections
Are A
Blessing

Your
Happiness
Depends
On You

Tough
Times
Never
Last

But
Tough
People
Do

There Is No Substitute For Hard Work

Learn As If You Were To Live Forever

Have
The
Courage
To
Continue

Be The
Friend
You Want
To Have

Own Your
Life Or
Someone
Else Will

Don't
Fear
Alone
Time

When
It Hurts
Observe

Life Is
Trying
To Tell
You
Something

Don't
Dwell
On The
Past

Don't
Feel The
World
Owes You

Don't
Expect
Quick
Results

Don't
Try To
Please
Everyone

Don't
Waste
Time

Feeling
Sorry
For
Yourself

Don't
Waste
Energy

On
Things
You
Cannot
Control

Don't
Let
Others

Influence
Your
Emotions

Don't
Resent
The
Success
Of Others

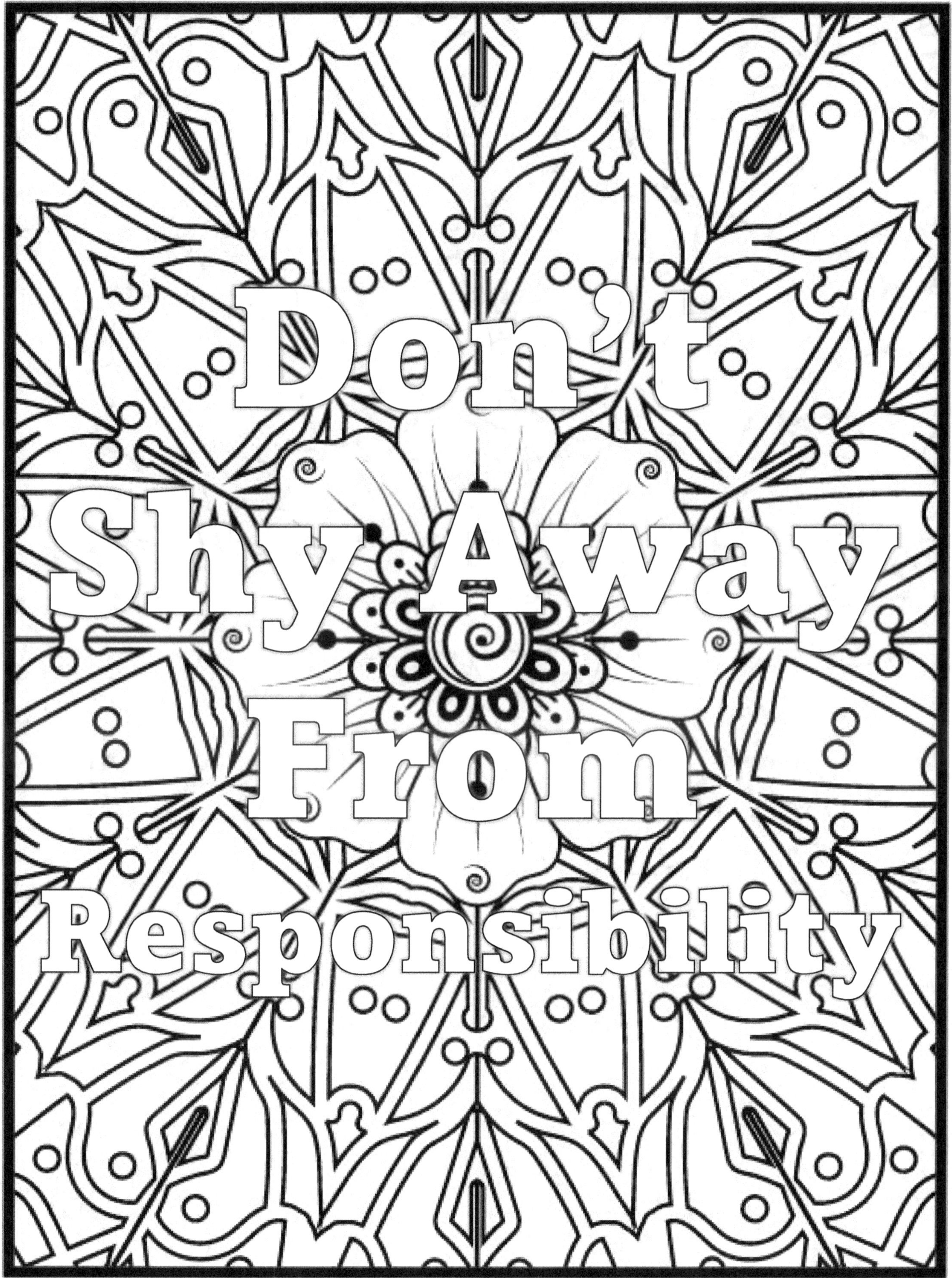

Don't
Shy Away
From
Responsibility

Don't
Give Up
After
Your
First
Failure

Don't
Fear
To Take
Risks

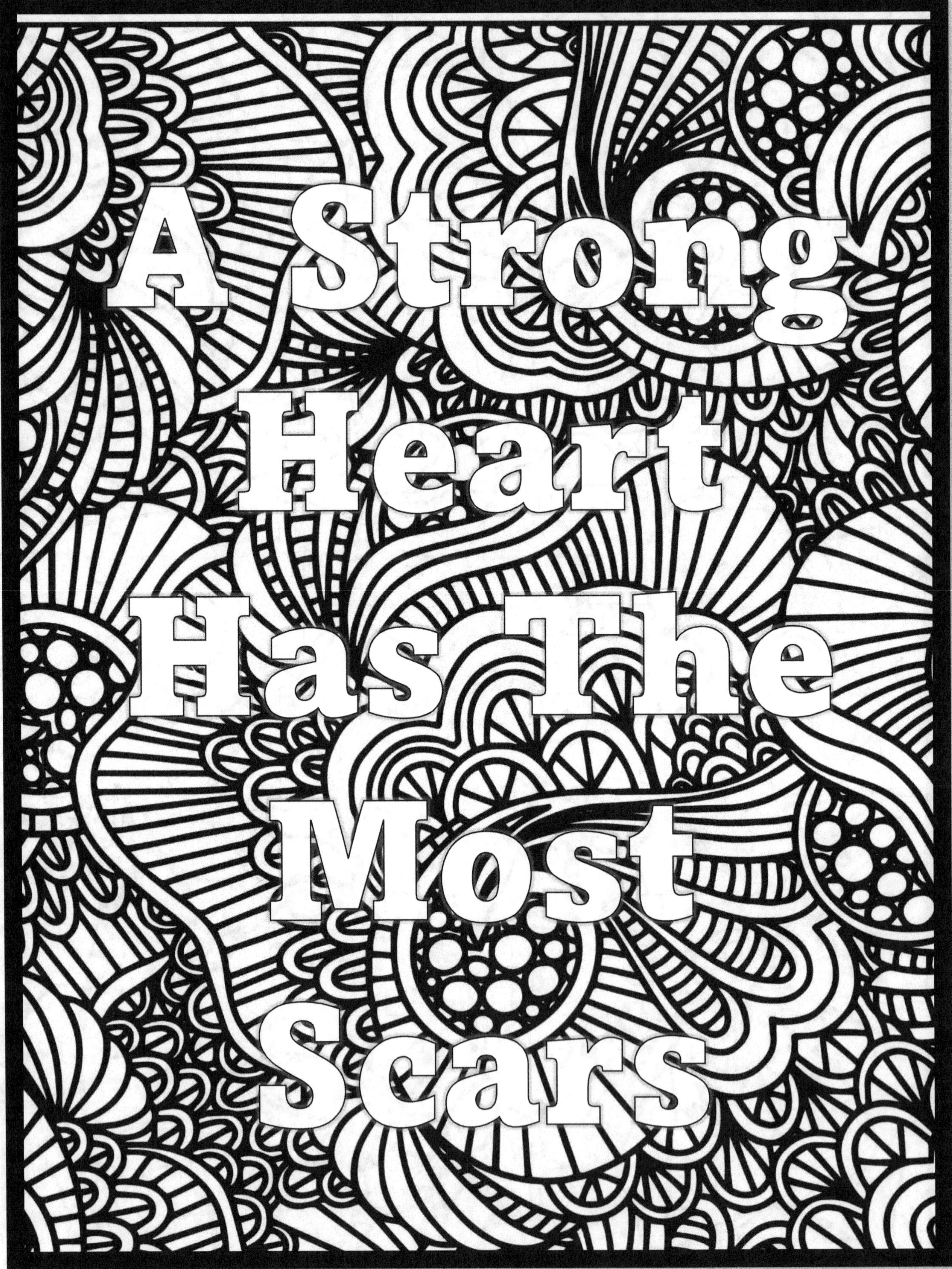
A Strong
Heart
Has The
Most
Scars

Your
Worth
Is
Measured
By

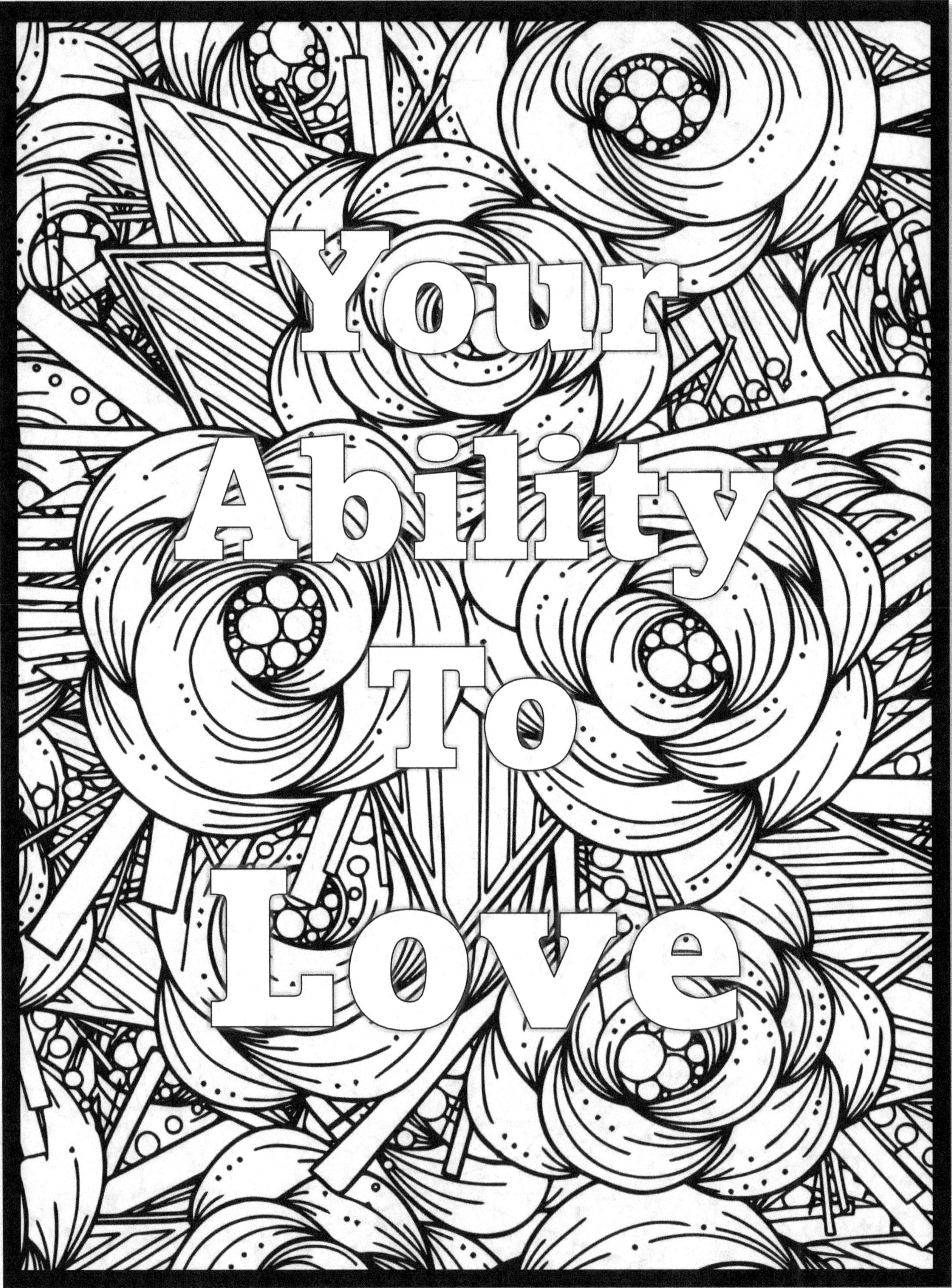
Your
Ability
To
Love

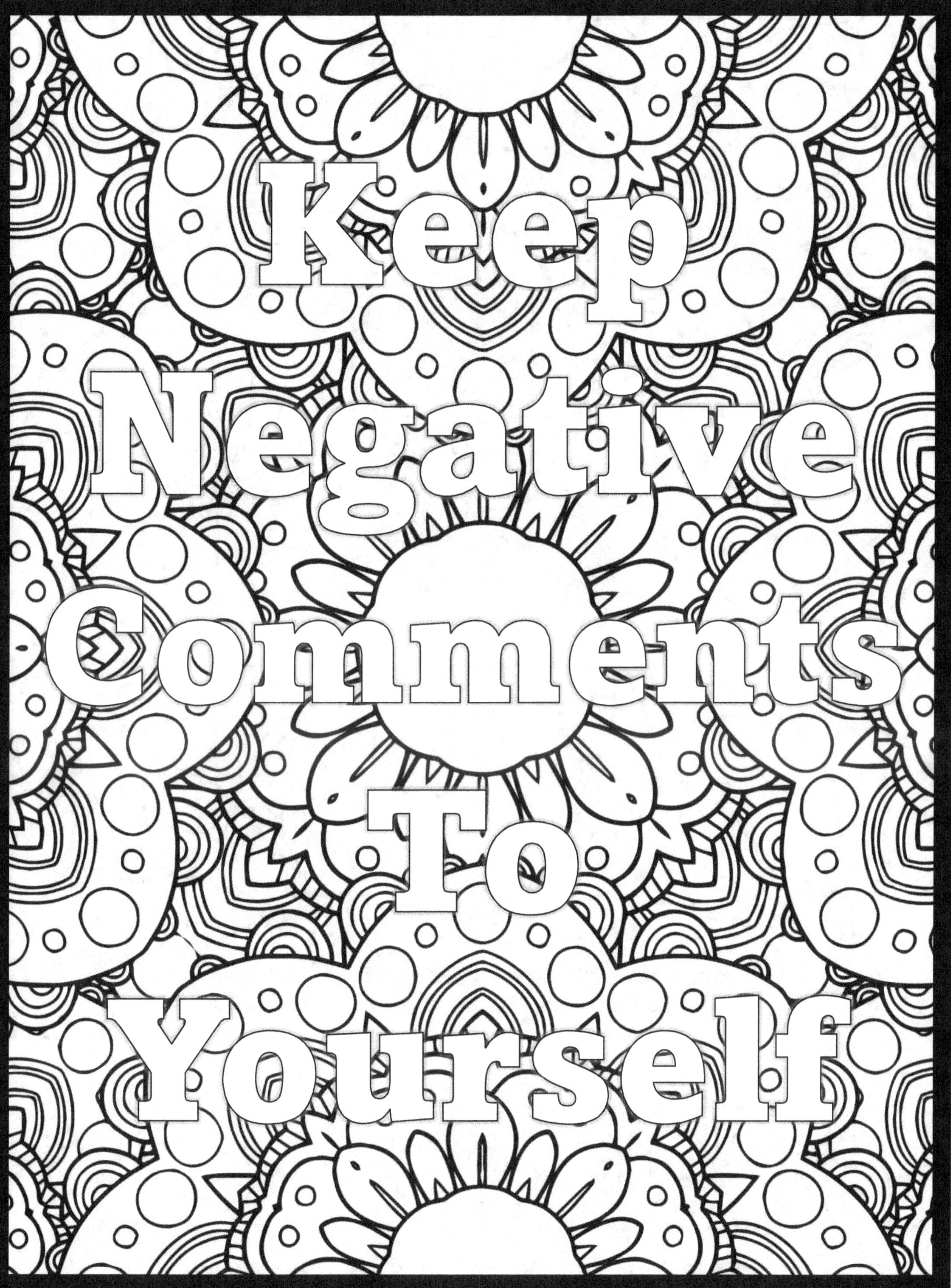

Keep
Negative
Comments
To
Yourself

Be
Kind
Be
Positive

Lead
By
Example

Be
Strong
Enough
To Stand
Alone

Consistent Hard Work Leads To Success

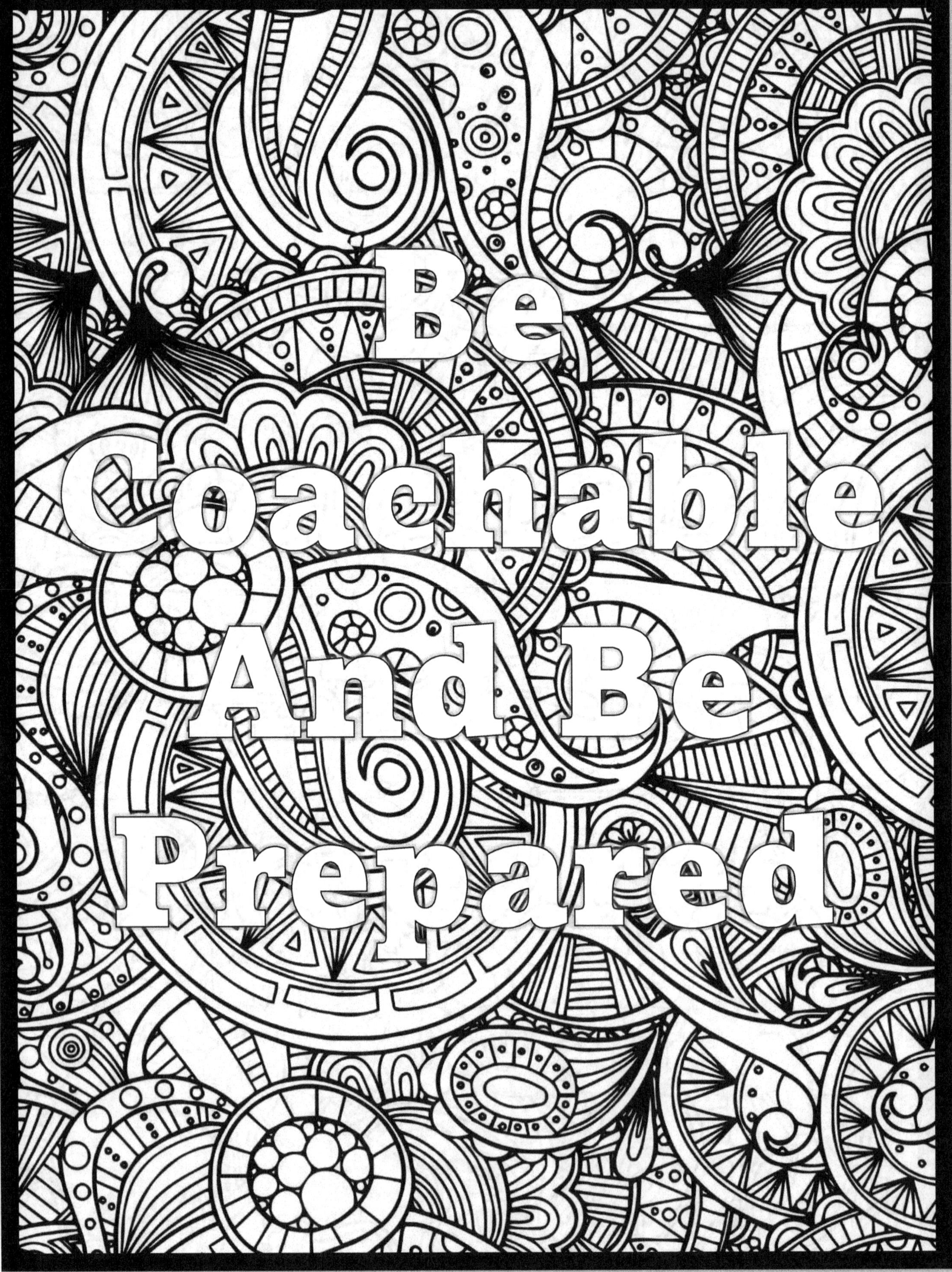

Be
Coachable
And Be
Prepared

Do A
Little
Extra
For
Others

The
Problem
Is How
We
React

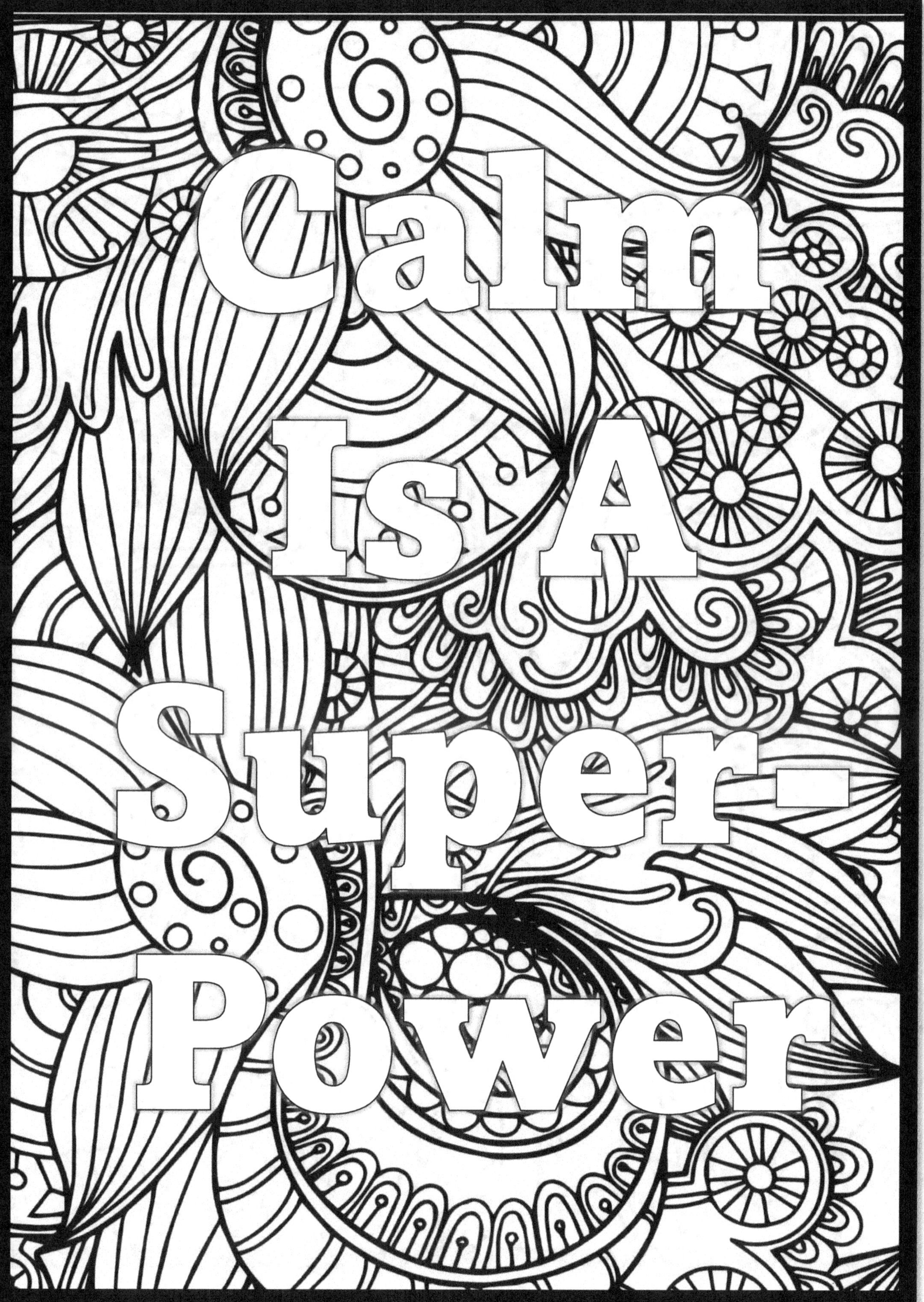
Calm Is A Super-Power

Patience
Is
Power

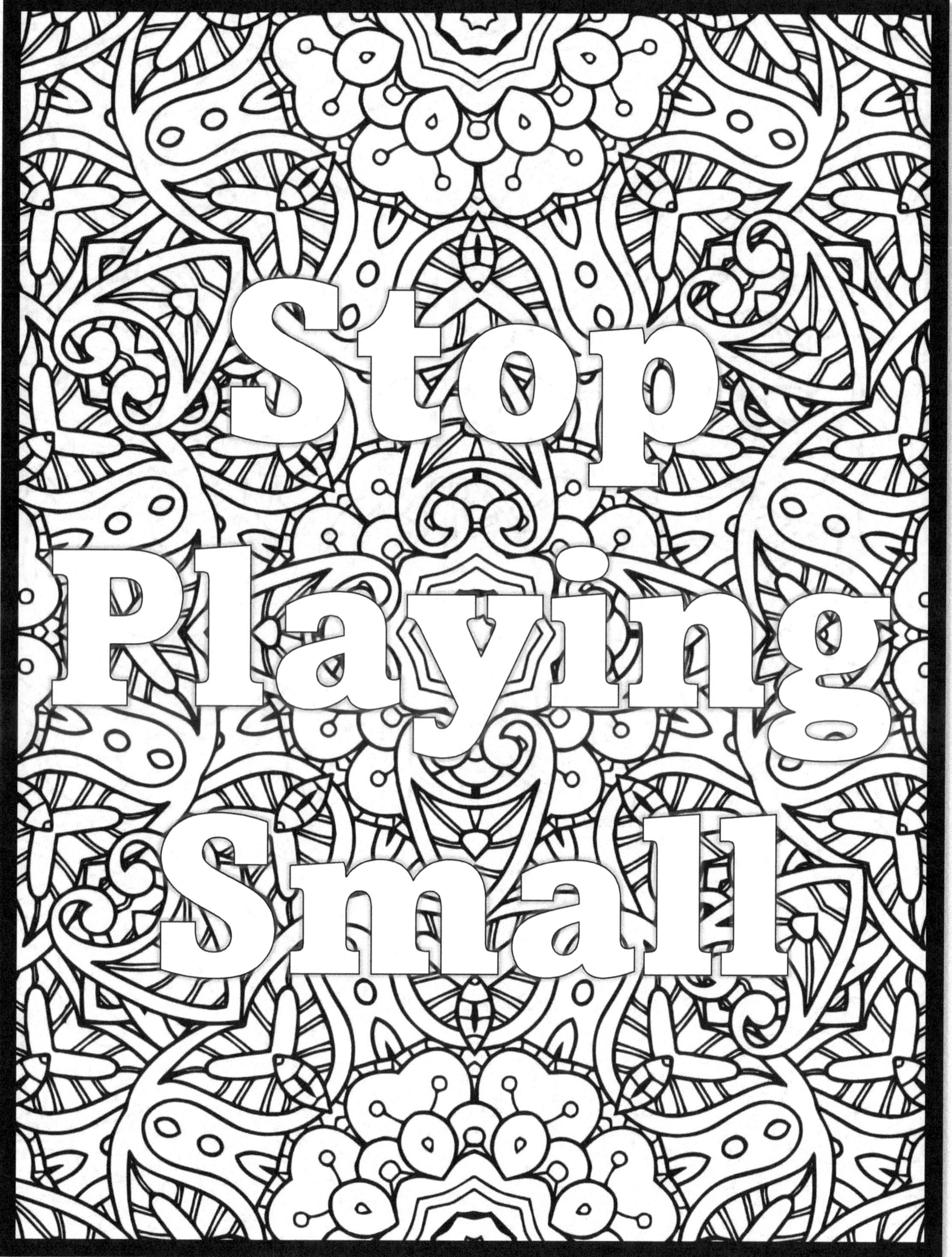

Stop
Playing
Small

You Are Meant To do Great Things

Feed
Your
Focus

You Can Learn Something From Everyone

Be
Good
To
Yourself

Learn To Admit Your Mistakes

It Is Not
Over
When
You Lose

It Is
Over
When
You
Quit

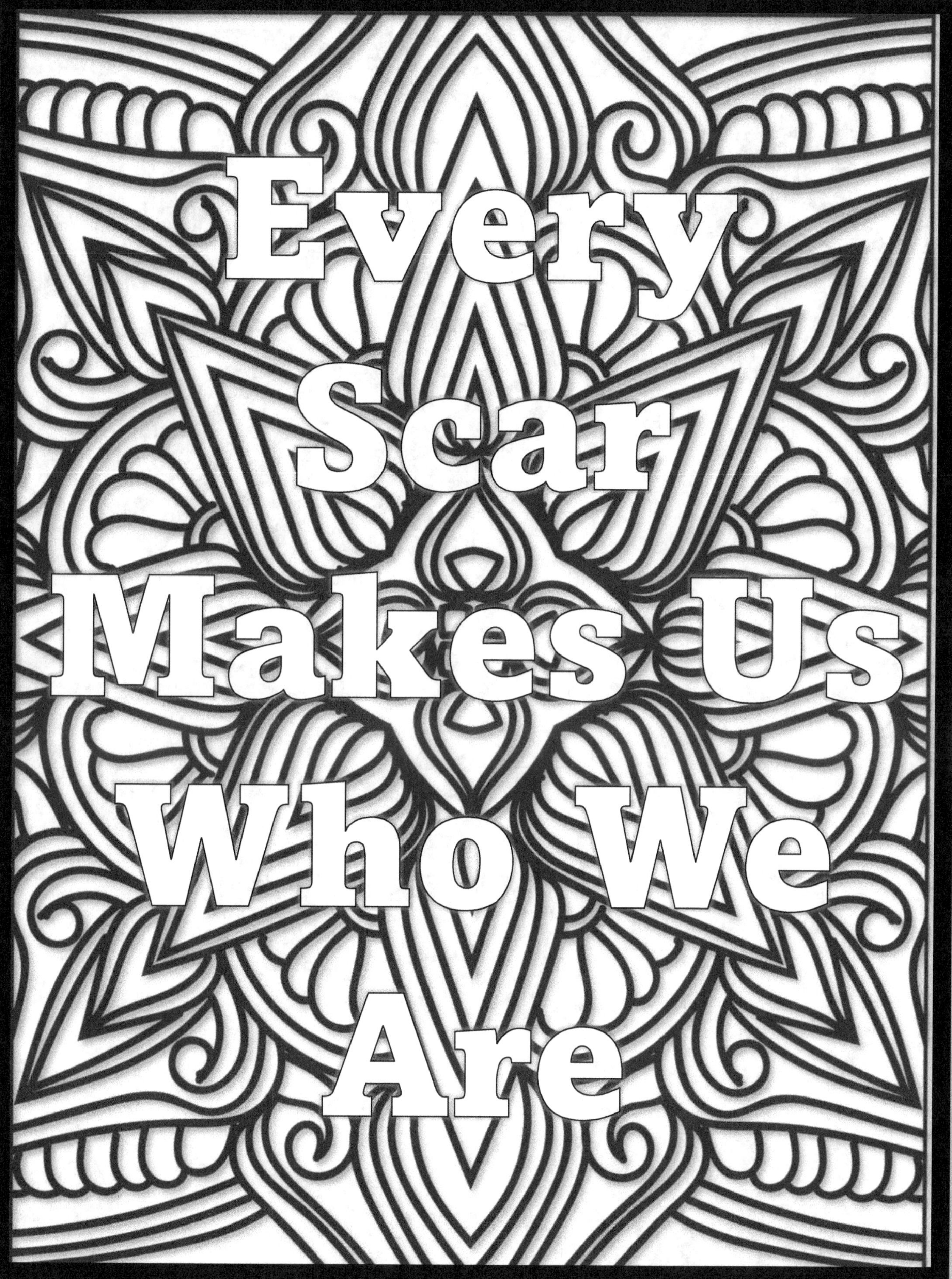
Every
Scar
Makes Us
Who We
Are

Do
It
Now

Hard
Does Not
Mean
Impossible

Fear
Is A
Choice

Never
Let The
Fire Die
Inside Of
You

You Are
Beautiful
You Are
Strong